Holidays
Labor Day

by Erika S. Manley

Bullfrog Books

Ideas for Parents and Teachers

Bullfrog Books let children practice reading informational text at the earliest reading levels. Repetition, familiar words, and photo labels support early readers.

Before Reading

- Discuss the cover photo. What does it tell them?
- Look at the picture glossary together. Read and discuss the words.

Read the Book

- "Walk" through the book and look at the photos. Let the child ask questions. Point out the photo labels.
- Read the book to the child, or have him or her read independently.

After Reading

- Prompt the child to think more. Ask: Do you celebrate Labor Day? What do you do?

Bullfrog Books are published by Jump!
5357 Penn Avenue South
Minneapolis, MN 55419
www.jumplibrary.com

Library of Congress Cataloging-in-Publication Data

Names: Manley, Erika S., author.
Title: Labor day / by Erika S. Manley.
Description: Minneapolis, MN: Jump!, Inc., [2018]
Series: Holidays | Includes index.
Identifiers: LCCN 2017025734 (print)
LCCN 2017032380 (ebook) | ISBN 9781624966668 (ebook) | ISBN 9781620318348 (hardcover: alk. paper) | ISBN 9781620318355 (pbk.)
Subjects: LCSH: Labor day—Juvenile literature.
Classification: LCC HD7791 (ebook)
LCC HD7791 .M26 2017 (print) | DDC 364.264—dc23
LC record available at https://lccn.loc.gov/2017025734

Editors: Jenna Trnka & Jenny Fretland VanVoorst
Book Designer: Leah Sanders
Photo Researcher: Leah Sanders

Photo Credits: anilakkus/iStock, cover; kurhan/Shutterstock, 1; Dragon Images/Shutterstock, 3; michaeljung/iStock, 4, 24; Jose Luis Pelaez Inc/Getty, 5, 23tl; Dmitry Kalinovsky/Shutterstock, 6–7; Dave & Les Jacobs/Getty, 8–9, Kobby Dagan/Shutterstock, 10–11, 23bl; Monkey Business Images/Shutterstock, 12–13, 20–21; kali9/iStock, 14, 22bl; 23tr; gresei/Shutterstock, 15; Echo/Getty, 16–17; Deklofenak/iStock, 18; Africa Studio/Shutterstock, 19, 22tr, 23br; Nikodash/Shutterstock, 22tl; Minerva Studio/Shutterstock, 22br.

Printed in the United States of America at Corporate Graphics in North Mankato, Minnesota.

Table of Contents

What Is Labor Day?

Labor Day is a U.S. holiday.

It is the first Monday in September.

What do we
celebrate?

Hard work!

5

We honor workers.
They make our
country strong.

Cities hold special events.
Leaders make speeches.
They thank workers.

There are
parades, too.

Look!

A marching
band plays.

marching
band

11

Many people have
the day off.

They do not work.

They spend time
with family.

Ella goes to a picnic.

She eats a hot dog.
Yum!

15

Labor Day means summer is over.

Fall is here.

Soon school will start.

supplies

We get ready.

We shop for supplies.

19

Labor Day is
a special day.

What will
you do?

21

Different Kinds of Work

Secretaries perform tasks in an office, such as answering phones and organizing files.

Construction workers build things, such as homes and schools.

Food service workers serve food and beverages.

Doctors help treat sick or injured people.

Picture Glossary

labor
Services performed by workers for wages.

picnic
A meal eaten outdoors, often during a trip away from home.

marching band
A band that marches while playing instruments.

supplies
Items needed for a particular activity.

Index

To Learn More

Learning more is as easy as 1, 2, 3.

1) Go to www.factsurfer.com

2) Enter "LaborDay" into the search box.

3) Click the "Surf" button to see a list of websites.

With factsurfer.com, finding more information is just a click away.